Contents

All recipes in the book are for 4 people unless otherwise
stated. Use either all metric or all imperial measures, as
the two are not necessarily interchangeable.

Foreword

Fish and shellfish caught in the Mediterranean have a completely different flavour to any from other seas. I believe that it is the particular salt concentration, as well as other environmental factors and, of course, the sun which make the seafood so amazingly distinctive.

Italy has more than 2,000 miles of coastline and many islands, which provide marvellous fishing grounds for individual fishermen who go fishing daily, ensuring that the catch is still extremely fresh when it reaches the shore. Part of the catch is used locally and the rest is sent by refrigerated lorries to inland cities, such as Milano, Torino, Firenze and Bologna, to be turned into wonderful dishes.

Italy also has some of the biggest lakes in Europe – the remnants of the Ice Age, when the glaciers flowed from the Alps to the Po valley. Fish such as pike, carp, lavarello, trout and many others live in these lakes. They are mostly consumed locally, where they are central to the creation of truly excellent traditional recipes.

The coasts of Liguria and Tuscany are home to fish like red mullet, anchovies, along with molluscs and crustaceans. Campania is famous for squid, sea bass, octopus and – above all – clams or *vongole* – the main ingredient of *spaghetti vongole*, one of my favourite dishes.

Calabria and Sicily offer the best anchovies in Italy, but also provide big fish such as swordfish and tuna. These areas are also responsible for a large fish canning industry.

On the Adriatic coast, Puglia and Marche are more famous for varieties of shellfish, like oysters, mussels, clams, sea dates, sea truffles and sea urchins. Perhaps the most outstanding piece of coastline is the Venetian Lagoon – there you can find the best cuttlefish, used especially for the production of black ink for *risotti*, along with spider crabs, clams, prawns, calamari, mussels, anchovies and red mullet. As you can imagine, fish is very much a part of Venetian cooking and in local restaurants all of these specialities are on offer.

As far as I know, Italy is one of the few countries in which, by law, you have to declare on menus if the fish is freshly caught or frozen. I find that this leads to more honesty among chefs with regard to ingredients.

In Italy it is strange that alongside so much fresh and frozen fish (the latter mostly used commercially), salt-cured and air-dried fish, originally from Norway, are also popular. Called *baccalà* and *stoccafisso* respectively, their use in Italy possibly dates from the expeditions of Columbus and other explorers, who used such 'everlasting' fish among their ships' provisions for long voyages. It then became used by the poor and by communities living away from the usual fresh-food supply routes. Today we are seeing a fashionable revival of salt cod because of its distinctive flavour, it is cooked both in restaurants and at home, consequently this resurgence of *baccalà* has driven prices higher.

In Italy we eat fish in many different ways: as an ingredient for delicious pasta sauces, in wonderful fish soups or stews, fried in batter or pan-fried in oil, steamed, grilled, baked in sea salt or sea water, or even eaten raw (cured with lemon juice and oil, or as a carpaccio, see page 25). An ancient way of eating fish is to use smoked tuna or swordfish; in Sardinia and Sicily these are used – together with *bottarga* (the salted or air-dried roe of either mullet or tuna) either to flavour pasta dishes or in thin slices with oil and lemon juice as an *apéritif*. In fact, while it is sold for a lot of money in other parts of Italy and abroad, this speciality is still a favourite among ancient fishermen sitting in front of the *trattoria* or *cantina* at the port, sipping a glass of white wine and enjoying slices of *bottarga*, as they have done for centuries and where locally it is considered a very simple snack.

In this book I will show you how we Italians like to eat our fish – mostly in uncomplicated recipes and always bursting with flavour. Remember that if you use the best fresh fish you can afford (following the advice of a good fishmonger), you will be well on the way to creating fantastic and memorable fish dishes!

Buying Fish

Good fresh fish remains the highest prize and it is therefore important to know what you are looking for when you buy it. It is crucial to have some knowledge of the flesh of the type of fish you are buying so you know the exact characteristics you are looking for and then, of course, to know the best way to cook it in order to make the most of both the dish and the fish.

It is essential that a fish is at its absolute freshest when it is bought so the first priority is to find a trustworthy supplier. Good indications of freshness for whole fish are clear, bright eyes and bright red gills. It is also important that it smells of the sea and that it does not smell of fish; this is a sure sign that it is old and will not taste fresh. Finally, the flesh of the fish should be firm to the touch, springing back to its former shape when touched. Some fish like tuna and swordfish are, however, 'hung' like game to develop the flavour and tenderness of the flesh.

If buying shellfish, the main point to look for is that the shells of molluscs such as mussels, clams and scallops are tightly closed. If they are even very slightly open, and don't close when tapped sharply on a hard surface, they are dead and should not be used. Other shellfish like crabs and lobster should be heavy and fresh-smelling. If they smell of fish it means they are not fresh, so reject them.

Above all, when buying seafood, trust your instincts and do not be afraid to reject anything that does not look, feel or smell right. Good fish, when it is fresh and well cooked, is a wonderful experience. It is no surprise that it has been such a staple part of the Mediterranean diet for so long and reassuring that its popularity is developing once again all over the world.

Preserving Fish

Bottling Anchovies

Fresh anchovies are layered in coarse sea salt, weighted and left for 3 months. During this time they exude oil, which is skimmed off regularly and the brine is topped up. They are judged 'ripe' when they develop a pleasant smell and a good pink colour.

Then comes the rinsing process to wash away excess salt and oil. The first rinse takes place in brine at 80°C (175°F); the second in fresh brine at 40°C (105°F); and the last in cold water. The fish are then filleted by hand, wrapped in porous cloths and put in a centrifugal spinner for 2–3 minutes to eliminate excess water. They are then carefully packed by hand into jars and covered with olive or vegetable oil.

Despite having a healthy supply of fresh and saltwater fish all over the country, Italy – like Spain and Portugal – also uses a great deal of *baccalà* and stockfish in its cooking. Both are forms of preserved cod; *baccalà* being salted at sea and then dried in large chunks when it is landed, and stockfish being whole air-dried fish. One or the other is eaten in all the regions of Italy, partly for economic reasons and partly for religious ones. It used to be the fish of the poor, and was eaten on Fridays by fasting Catholics who did not have access to fresh fish. Now, though, it is valued for its distinctive flavour and versatility.

Other fish preserved in salt include anchovies and sardines, both of which have given birth to many dishes. Preserved anchovies are particularly valued, being used in a huge number of dishes – from the ancient Roman condiment *garum* to today's pizza. Fish are also pickled in vinegar and this gives the flesh of freshwater fish like carp, goregone, eels and trout an almost Oriental sweet-and-sour tang.

Another traditional method of preserving fish is by smoke-curing it. In Italy, this method was used in the past only for meat such as hams, but in top restaurants it is now possible to be served very thinly sliced smoked swordfish, tuna fish and sturgeon, as well as air-dried and salted cod or mullet roe (known as bottarga), a very expensive speciality from Sardinia and Sicily. Salted and air-dried fillets of tuna fish, known as *mosciame*, are a delicacy to compare with the finest of foods, while the smoked swordfish, tuna and sturgeon are of a high enough quality to be exported to the connoisseurs of fish in the Nordic countries, alongside their locally smoked salmon, mackerel, eel and herring.

Opposite: Mosciame (left) and Bottarga di Tonno (see Tuna Fish, page 31)

Insalata di Aringhe, Arance e Pompelmi
SALAD OF SMOKED HERRING, ORANGE AND GRAPEFRUIT

2 pink grapefruit

4 oranges

1 red onion, cut into thin rings

4 smoked herring fillets, thinly sliced

4 tbsp extra-virgin olive oil

2 tsp white wine vinegar

freshly ground black pepper

fennel fronds, to decorate

Herring
This North Atlantic fish is not caught in the Mediterranean but is widely used in Italy, generally in antipasto, *once it has been salt-cured and smoked. One of the most remarkable recipes for it I have tasted comes from Sicily, where it is eaten in a salad with grapefruit and orange.*

Peel the grapefruit and oranges, removing all the white pith, then cut out the segments from between the membranes. Do this over a bowl to catch the juice, then squeeze out any juice from the membranes. Arrange the fruit segments on a plate and scatter over the onion rings, then arrange the herring slices next to them.

Add the oil, vinegar and some pepper to the grapefruit and orange juice to make a vinaigrette. Mix well and pour over the salad, then decorate with fennel fronds. Serve with good bread.

This typically refreshing Sicilian recipe probably came about as a way of using the abundant crops of citrus fruit and the smoked herrings that would have been brought to the island by visiting ships.

Polenta e Baccalà

POLENTA AND SALT COD

Salt Cod

Two regions of Italy are famous for their baccalà *recipes, Liguria and the Veneto. In the past it was the food of the poor and was especially useful because it could be eaten on religious fast days in the land-locked valleys of the Alps where access to fresh fish was difficult. Today, as with many other traditional peasant foods, it is enjoying a renaissance in Italian cuisine.*

Baccalà, or salt cod, can only be used after having been soaked in frequent changes of fresh water for at least 24 hours to soften the flesh and remove the salt.

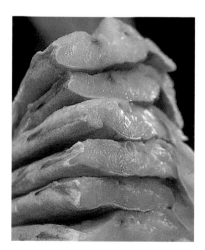

1.5 kg (3¼ lb) salt cod, taken from the middle part of the fish

175 ml (6 fl oz) extra-virgin olive oil

1 onion, finely sliced

2 garlic cloves, coarsely chopped

400 g (14 oz) tin of chopped tomatoes, or 3 large ripe tomatoes, peeled and coarsely chopped

8 basil leaves

3 tbsp coarsely chopped flat-leaf parsley

1 glass of red wine

salt and pepper

FOR THE POLENTA:

25 g (¾ oz) salt

300 g (10½ oz) coarse polenta

Cut the cod into smallish pieces and soak in cold water for 36 hours, changing the water every 6 hours. Drain and remove the bones and fins; cut the cod into chunks.

For the polenta, bring 2 litres (3½ pints) of water and the salt to the boil in a heavy-based pan. Sift the polenta through your hand into the water, stirring constantly to avoid lumps. Cook for 40 minutes, stirring all the time, until it pulls away from the sides of the pan.

Heat 125 ml (4 fl oz) of the olive oil in a pan, add the onion and garlic and fry until soft. Add the tomatoes and herbs and simmer until the sauce begins to thicken. Heat the remaining oil in a separate pan and fry the cod in it for 6–7 minutes on each side. Pour the tomato sauce and wine on top, season with pepper (and salt if necessary) and cook gently for 20 minutes, then serve with the polenta.

Involtini di Pesce Spada

STUFFED SWORDFISH ROLLS

8 slices of swordfish, 1 cm (½ inch) thick, more or less the same shape

3 tbsp fresh breadcrumbs

8 black olives, stoned and finely chopped

pinch of fresh or dried oregano

3 tbsp coarsely chopped flat-leaf parsley

4 tbsp olive oil

600 g (1 lb 5 oz) polpa di pomodoro (tomato pulp)

salt and pepper

Put the slices of swordfish on top of each other and cut off the pieces sticking out to obtain equal-shaped slices. Finely chop the trimmings.

Make the filling by mixing the breadcrumbs with the olives, oregano, parsley, swordfish trimmings and some salt and pepper. Place the mixture in the centre of each swordfish slice, roll up and secure with a toothpick. Heat the olive oil in a pan, add the swordfish rolls and fry gently for 5 minutes on each side until cooked through. Remove the swordfish from the pan and set aside.

Put the tomatoes in the same pan and simmer for 5 minutes. Add salt to taste, return the fish to the pan and warm through. Remove the toothpicks and serve.

Swordfish

Sicily is one of the largest consumers of swordfish. It is one of those fish that are generally hung for at least one day before use. The flesh is very similar in texture, colour and taste to that of shark meat and for this reason is cut and cooked in a similar way. It is mostly grilled but more recently it has been served raw as carpaccio and smoked. One of the most interesting ways to cook swordfish is in involtini di pesce spada.

This recipe is typical of Sicily, where swordfish is regarded as a speciality. Almost every family has its own filling but the result is always extremely tasty.

Bagna Caôda

HOT ANCHOVY AND GARLIC DIP

125 g (4½ oz) butter
6 garlic cloves, crushed
300 g (10½ oz) anchovy fillets (best if taken from salted anchovies)
200 ml (7 fl oz) extra-virgin olive oil
mixed raw vegetables, to serve (see right)

Put the butter and garlic in a terracotta pot over a very gentle flame and leave, stirring occasionally, until the garlic has dissolved in the hot, but not boiling, butter. Add the anchovy fillets and the oil and continue to cook extremely gently until the mixture becomes creamy.

The bagna caôda is now ready to be enjoyed by dipping the vegetables in it.

This is usually enjoyed with friends, sharing a common terracotta pot which is kept warm over a candle. Special pots for individual portions are also available.

Serving Bagna Caôda

There are many versions of this hot Piedmontese dip, which is served with raw vegetables. The vegetables must be extremely fresh and tender, all cut into strips. Choose from cardoons, Jerusalem artichokes (cleaned and cut into thin slices), red and yellow peppers, raw cauliflower florets, celery stalks, artichoke hearts, spring onions, or whatever else is available. Abundant bread! Abundant wine to drink!

Sardine in Carpione
MARINATED SWEET-AND-SOUR SARDINES

12 large fresh sardines, cleaned

flour for dusting

olive oil for frying

FOR THE MARINADE:

1 large onion, thinly sliced

1 tomato, deseeded and sliced

2 bay leaves

2 tbsp raisins

1 tbsp pine nuts

1 small chilli

90 ml (3 fl oz) olive oil

5 tbsp white wine vinegar

1 small glass of dry white wine

1 tsp sugar

Dust the sardines in flour, then shallow-fry them in olive oil until crisp on both sides. Arrange them in a single layer in a shallow dish.

For the marinade, fry the onion, tomato, bay leaves, raisins, pine nuts and chilli in the oil until the vegetables are soft. Stir in the vinegar, wine and sugar and pour the marinade over the warm fish. Leave to marinate for a few hours before serving.

This is a delightful summer dish which can be served as an *antipasto*.

The fish should be very fresh.

Sardine

Sardines are relatively fatty and the simplest way to eat them is brushed with a little lemon juice, olive oil, parsley, garlic, salt and pepper and then grilled. They can also be boned and stuffed or dipped in flour, egg and breadcrumbs and deep-fried.

The Sicilians honour the sardine in two special ways; firstly using it as a sauce for pasta and secondly as sardine a beccafico, *which are fillets of sardines rolled and stuffed with breadcrumbs, pine kernels and raisins mixed in olive oil and then baked in the oven and served with a sprinkling of orange juice.*

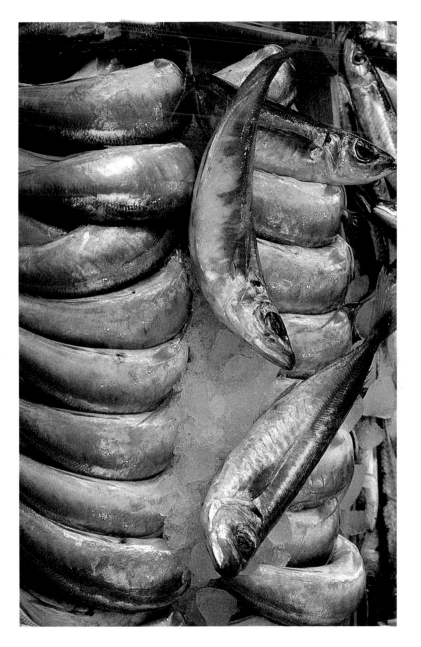

Lavarello e Trota Marinate

MARINATED LAKE FISH OR TROUT

4 tbsp extra-virgin olive oil

juice of 2 lemons

finely grated zest of ½ lemon

1 tsp sugar

1 tbsp finely grated horseradish

600 g (1¼ lb) lake bream or trout fillet cut from a large fish,
    very thinly sliced

2 tbsp very finely chopped flat-leaf parsley

salt and pepper

To make the marinade, beat together the oil, lemon juice and zest,
sugar, horseradish and salt and pepper to taste. Lay the slices of fish on
a non-metallic plate. Spread the marinade over the fish and leave for a
couple of hours, then turn the fish over and cover with the marinade
that has not been absorbed. Sprinkle with the parsley and serve with
bread or *grissini* as an *antipasto*.

Lavarello

*These very versatile lake fish can be cooked
in many ways: they may be fried and
marinated to make an excellent appetizer,
or cut into fillets, dusted with flour, dotted
with butter and sprinkled with sage leaves
then baked in the oven. The modern way is
to serve them raw, thinly sliced, which is
known as carpaccio.*

Only extremely fresh fish are suitable for this
uncooked dish. The fillets are 'cooked' by the
acid of the lemon juice in the marinade.

Anguilla alla Luciana
EEL BAKED WITH BAY LEAVES

Eel

Eels are traditionally eaten fried, grilled, baked and stewed. In Sardinia, they are cooked with tomatoes. One of the most memorable dishes I have had with eel was one in which it was simply baked with bay leaves and no other flavouring (see right).

The capitone, *a large female eel which has reached its maximum weight, is perhaps worth a special mention. It is traditionally eaten at Christmas and is a delicacy in Rome and all over the South. The fish is cut into sections, cured with olive oil, garlic, mint and vinegar, then grilled on charcoal.*

1 large eel, weighing about 1.25 kg (2½ lb), or 2 weighing 800 g (1¾ lb) each
about 24 freshly picked large bay leaves
coarse salt

Preheat the oven to 200°C/400°F/gas 6. Kill and skin the eel if your fishmonger has not already done so. Gut the eel and rub with a cloth to remove some of the shine. Cut into 7.5 cm (3 inch) chunks and layer in a terracotta pot, adding some bay leaves and coarse salt between each layer. Bake, uncovered, for 30–40 minutes, depending on the size of the eel – test with a skewer to see if it is done.
Serves 6–8

The brilliant results belie the simplicity of this recipe. The eel has to be alive, or freshly killed by the fishmonger.

Spiedino di Grandi Pesci

SKEWERS OF FISH

1 kg (2¼ lb) mixed fish fillets (see below), cut into large cubes

FOR THE MARINADE:

juice of 1 lemon

1 small glass of white wine

1 tbsp balsamic vinegar

3 tbsp extra virgin olive oil

1 tbsp finely chopped parsley

1 tbsp finely chopped sage

1 tbsp finely chopped mint

salt and pepper

Make the marinade by mixing all the ingredients together. Put the fish in a bowl and pour over the marinade. Leave for a few hours.

Thread chunks of alternate types of fish on to 4 long skewers and grill for 3–5 minutes, depending on the size of the chunks, on each side over a charcoal grill, on a ridged cast iron pan or under a domestic grill. Baste with the marinade during cooking.

Serve with a rocket salad.

A fish merchant cutting up tuna and swordfish.

Cooking on a skewer works well if you choose chunks of large fish such as tuna, swordfish, large trout, salmon, turbot, halibut or monkfish.

Tuna Fish

Fresh tuna is eaten in a similar way to swordfish, sliced and usually grilled as a steak, or cooked with tomato sauce. Tuna can be eaten raw like carpaccio, providing the meat is very fresh, and can also be eaten as mosciame – air-dried fillets. Ventresca, or the belly of the tuna, was often salted in barrels or canned as a particular delicacy. When tuna roes are salted and air-dried they are known as bottarga di tonno.

Branzino all'Acqua di Mare
SEA BASS COOKED IN SEA WATER

2 sea bass, weighing about 500 g (1 lb) each, cleaned

equal quantities of sea water (see right), dry white wine and
   extra-virgin olive oil (enough to reach the belly of the fish in the pan)

juice of 1 lemon

1 tbsp parsley leaves

1 tbsp oregano leaves

black pepper

Put the fish in a large pan with all the remaining ingredients. Cover the
pan and bring to the boil. Remove the lid, reduce the heat and simmer
for 10 minutes. Turn the fish over and simmer for a further 12 minutes
or until cooked through. Serve with boiled potatoes and a spoonful of
the cooking liquid.

A merchant at Venice's Rialto fish market.

Sea Bass

Sea bass, spigola or branzino, is often baked
whole in a salt crust or in foil parcels with
parsley, garlic, lemon and fennel. The
Sicilians cook it in sea water, as in this
recipe. Naturally it should be unpolluted
sea water if you can find it. Otherwise use
ordinary water and salt.

When Italians hear the words *spigola* or *branzino* their culinary hearts start to beat a little faster, for sea bass is one of the best-loved fish in Italy.

Cacciucco

This classic Livornese fish soup, also called buridda *in Liguria, is made using a wide variety of fish, but usually includes* murena *(moray eel) and* scorfano *(scorpion fish), with wine, garlic, parsley, olive oil and tomatoes.*

Cacciucco

LIVORNESE FISH STEW

500 g (1 lb) scorpion fish (if you can find it)
500 g (1 lb) monkfish
225 g (8 oz) octopus
225 g (8 oz) squid
225 g (8 oz) clams
6 tomatoes, chopped
salt and pepper
olive oil for frying
FOR THE STOCK:
1 large onion, chopped
1–2 carrots, chopped
2 celery stalks, chopped
chunk of wild fennel, chopped
2–3 bay leaves
12 black peppercorns

First clean and prepare the fish and shellfish. Set aside the good pieces. To make the stock, put the fish trimmings in a large pan with the onion, carrots, celery, fennel, bay leaves and peppercorns. Add enough water to cover and then simmer very gently for 20 minutes.

Meanwhile heat a layer of olive oil in a large pan, add the pieces of white fish, octopus and squid and fry gently on each side for about a minute. Add the tomatoes. Strain the fish stock and pour in the pan to cover the fish. Simmer for about 3 minutes, then add the clams and cook for a further 2 minutes, until the shells have opened. Season with salt and pepper and serve immediately.
Serves 6

Stocco alla Genovese
STOCKFISH STEW

1 kg (2¼ lb) stockfish or salt cod

90 ml (3 fl oz) extra-virgin olive oil

1 large onion, finely chopped

about 20 tasty black olives, ideally Ligurian Taggiasca

2 garlic cloves, coarsely chopped

4 anchovy fillets

85 g (3 oz) toasted pine nuts

2 tbsp coarsely chopped flat-leaf parsley

black pepper

Soak the stockfish in cold water overnight, then drain, cover with fresh water and bring to the boil. Reduce the heat and simmer for 2–2½ hours, until tender. Drain and remove the flesh from the bones.

Heat the olive oil in a pan and fry the onion in it until soft. Add the olives, garlic and anchovies and cook for 5 minutes. Stir in the fish, pine nuts and parsley and cook for a further 5 minutes, then season to taste with black pepper. Serve with polenta (see page 16).

Stockfish

Stockfish is air-dried and sold whole. Although it is unsalted, it requires lengthy soaking before cooking to rehydrate, as well as vigorous beating with a mallet in order to tenderize it and break up the fibres. Strangely, it is called baccalà *(the term generally used for salt cod, see page 16) in Vicenza and Venice although it is known as stoccafisso elsewhere in Italy. In fact Vicenza is famous for its* baccalà alle vicentina *which is usually eaten with white polenta.*

If you can find them, the Ligurian Taggiasca olives really impart a wonderful flavour to the dish.

Triglie alle Olive

RED MULLET WITH OLIVES

Red Mullet

Probably one of my favourite fish, especially the rock mullet (Mullus surmuletus) when it is no more than 15 cm (6 inches) long and deep-fried after being dusted in flour. It is very delicate, easily perishable and it offers one of the greatest treats if it is cooked within a day of being caught. It is impossible to freeze or preserve it in other ways.

Red mullet is excellent baked, fried or grilled, or used in fish soups where it should be added at the last minute to avoid overcooking. Larger fish are often filleted to remove the numerous bones. It can also be eaten in a pasta sauce and the best I have ever tasted was pasta con le triglie *cooked by Pinuccia of the restaurant S. Giovanni at Casarza in Liguria.*

3 tbsp extra-virgin olive oil

8 whole fresh red mullet, each weighing about 125 g (4½ oz), or 4 weighing about 250 g (9 oz), cleaned and scaled

1 garlic clove, finely chopped

3 tbsp finely chopped parsley

85 g (3 oz) small tasty black olives, finely chopped

4 anchovy fillets, coarsely chopped

4 tbsp passata

200 g (7 oz) tomatoes, peeled, deseeded and cubed

salt and pepper

Heat the olive oil in a pan and fry the fish for 4 minutes on each side if small or 6–8 minutes if larger. Remove from the pan with a slotted spoon and set aside.

Add the garlic, parsley and olives to the pan and cook gently for 2 or 3 minutes, then add the anchovies. Stir until the anchovies dissolve to a purée.

Add the passata, followed by the tomatoes. Bring to a simmer and return the fish to the pan. Cook for 5 minutes each side. Season to taste and serve warm.

Freshness is the most important aspect of every fish, but for red mullet in particular it is essential.

Insalata di Mare
SEAFOOD SALAD

Octopus

There is a famous stand in the middle of the Vucceria market in Palermo, Sicily, where you can eat freshly cooked and locally caught polpo *(octopus) from an old aluminium pot. Into the boiling water goes the fresh, creamy-coloured octopus and after a few minutes out it comes, extremely tender and an appetizing pinky-red. It is cut up on the stall so that it can be eaten straight away. It does not need to be accompanied by any sauces or spices; nature has already provided all the essential ingredients.*

Octopus can be eaten in salads or freshly poached, affogato, *as in Naples, or by cooking in a covered pot with some oil, garlic, tomatoes, olives, chilli and parsley for about 30 minutes.*

Similar to the polpo *is the smaller* moscardino, *which has only one row of suckers on its tentacles and is not so well appreciated in the kitchen although it is still very good. The same recipes can be used for both, as long as an adjustment is made in the cooking time for the* moscardino's *smaller size.*

2 garlic cloves, cut in half

juice of 2 lemons

600 g (1 ¼ lb) mixed seafood, such as prawns, mussels, small octopuses, small squid (or large ones cut into rings), clams, or whatever you find at the fishmonger's, cleaned

90 ml (3 fl oz) olive oil

2 tbsp finely chopped flat-leaf parsley

salt and pepper

Put the garlic in the lemon juice and leave for about an hour, then discard the garlic when the juice has taken on its aroma. Meanwhile, cook the shellfish in a little water in a covered pan for a few minutes until the shells open. Remove and discard all the shells. Simmer all the other fish in a large pan of water until just cooked and then drain.

Mix the lemon juice with the olive oil, parsley, and salt and pepper to taste. Mix this dressing with the fish, then leave to rest and cool.

Mix again, then serve as an *antipasto* with bread or *grissini*.

As with most Italian dishes, the taste of this salad depends on the freshness of the seafood rather than on herbs and spices.

Capasante al Burro e Limone
SCALLOPS WITH BUTTER AND LEMON

12 large scallops, with the corals attached
55 g (1¾ oz) butter
juice of ½ lemon
about 2 tbsp fish stock
1 tbsp finely chopped flat-leaf parsley
salt and pepper
flour for dusting

Dust the scallops with flour. Heat the butter in a pan, add the scallops and fry for 2 minutes on each side. Remove from the pan and set aside. Add the lemon juice and stock to the pan, stirring to scrape up the sediment from the bottom. If necessary add a little more stock. Stir in the parsley and some salt and pepper. Return the scallops to the pan, heat through briefly and serve.

A discerning shopper at Venice's Rialto fish market.

Scallops

Some of the best recipes have evolved from Venice, including risotto ai canestrelli, *an Italian version of Spanish* paella, *although the finest scallops are rightly reserved for a simple but exquisite seafood salad. The fine flavour of the scallop suits the simplest of treatments, say with a little white wine, garlic and parsley.*

Scallops are one of the most delicate of shellfish. They should be cooked briefly, either by frying or poaching.

Seppie al Nero
CUTTLEFISH IN ITS OWN SAUCE

Cuttlefish

The cuttlefish carries ink in its body which it ejects to confuse enemies when they are in pursuit. The famous sepia or black colour of its ink was in great use by artists at the time of Leonardo da Vinci and his contemporaries. Seppiette in nero con polenta is perhaps one of the most famous dishes made using the ink.

The striped skin is removed when the fish is prepared for cooking. The beak, eyes and innards (including the 'bone') are also removed and the black ink sac in the centre of the tentacles carefully removed and reserved. The ink may also be bought separately in sachets.

Like the squid, cuttlefish are often stuffed and baked or simply grilled or stewed in rich wine and/or tomato sauces.

700–800 g (1½ – 1¾ lb) fresh cuttlefish
90 ml (3 fl oz) olive oil
1 small onion, very finely chopped
1 small garlic clove, very finely chopped
1 small glass of dry white wine
1 red chilli, chopped (optional)
salt and pepper

Clean the cuttlefish very thoroughly (see left), detaching the small, silver-coloured ink sac and setting it aside. Cut off the tentacles and wash them.

Heat the oil in a large pan, add the onion and garlic and cook for a few minutes. Add the white wine and bubble for a few minutes to evaporate the alcohol, then add the cuttlefish and tentacles, cover the pan and cook gently for 20 minutes. Now add the black ink and dilute with a little water to make it liquid. Season with salt and pepper, add the chilli if using it, and cook for another 10 minutes or until the cuttlefish is tender.

Serve with boiled rice or with polenta and bread.

You must use cuttlefish for this recipe in order to have enough black ink. Squid and octopus also contain ink, but in less quantity.

Sauté Misto di Vongole e Datteri
MIXED SAUTÉ OF CLAMS AND SEA DATES

1 kg (2¼ lb) carpet shell clams
1 kg (2¼ lb) telline (wedge shell) clams
500 g (1 lb) sea dates or sea truffles
4 tbsp extra-virgin olive oil
1 garlic clove, finely chopped
225 g (8 oz) tomatoes, coarsely chopped
2 tbsp chopped flat-leaf parsley
black pepper

Thoroughly clean the shellfish under cold running water, discarding any that are open or that do not look very healthy.

Heat the olive oil in a large pan and briefly fry the garlic, ensuring that it does not change colour. Put all the shellfish and the tomatoes in the pan and cook with the lid on. After a few minutes the shells will open up. Keeping the lid on, shake the pan so that all the shells cook evenly. Check that all the shells have opened, then stir in the parsley and abundant freshly ground black pepper.

Serve on a plate with the lovely sea water sauce that comes from the seafood, which should be mopped up with very good bread. It is customary to eat this dish with your fingers, sucking out the meat from the shells. Provide finger bowls!

Everyone in the South likes this dish. You can use just one type of clam if that's all you can get.

Clam

Clams are also very good when eaten cooked on their own. Put some good olive oil, garlic, parsley and a little chilli in a pan with a little water. Heat to a high temperature then add the clams. Cover with a lid and steam for 5–6 minutes, or until all the shells have opened. I like to eat them straight from the shell with some good crusty bread to soak up the delicious juices.

Sea Date

The dattero di mare is very sought-after and a real delicacy. In Puglia and in the Gulf of Spezia, where it grows best, there are special laws to regulate their fishing. To catch them, you literally have to break the rock to which they are attached and the fishing boats need lifting tackle to heft the rocks on board. The practice is likely soon to be made illegal as it is ruining some stretches of coastline.

Provided you know where they come from, you can eat sea dates raw like oysters. Because of their unique habitat, unlike other mussels, they do not contain sand.

Calamaretti in Umido

SMALL BRAISED SQUID

Squid

To prepare calamari *and* calamaretti *for cooking, the skin is first removed. Then the transparent quill inside the tube is removed and discarded. The black ink sac inside the body should be removed carefully and reserved if you want to use it to colour a dish.*

Once cleaned, squid can be cooked in a variety of ways. They are often poached whole very briefly in sea water and eaten in salads dressed with olive oil and lemon. In Apulia, they use very little water for the broth and then drink it as a tonic after cooking the squid. Alternatively, whole small squid or large ones cut into rings are dusted with flour and deep-fried until crispy. They may also be grilled or stuffed whole as here.

breadcrumbs from 1 fresh bread roll

a little milk

600 g (1¼ lb) small squid, cleaned (see left)

1 garlic clove, very finely chopped

3 tbsp very finely chopped flat-leaf parsley

4 tbsp extra-virgin olive oil

2 large ripe tomatoes, peeled, deseeded and chopped

salt and pepper

Soak the breadcrumbs in a little milk to cover, then squeeze out the excess liquid. Cut off the tentacles from the squid. Chop the tentacles and mix them with the breadcrumbs, garlic, parsley and some salt and pepper. Stuff this mixture into the cavities of the squid, filling them about three-quarters full.

Heat the oil in a large pan and briefly fry the squid until they become slightly pinkish in colour. Add the chopped tomatoes and cook for about 15 minutes, until you obtain a lovely sauce.

When I bought the fish for this recipe in Pozzuoli, I was given a handful of seaweed, which I dipped in an extremely light batter and then fried very briefly to serve with the squid.

ALLA CARNE

...RRO CEFALÙ

...DE SALATE ALLA CARNE

...CE AZZURRO CEFALÙ

SARDE SALATE ALLA CAR...

AZZUR...

Glossary of Fish and Shellfish

Acciuga, Alice / *Anchovy*
Probably the best-loved and most versatile of Italian fish, anchovies are small saltwater fish which live in deep waters and approach the shore only during the spring mating season. The fishing of this speciality is strictly controlled to avoid damaging stocks. Being a lovely blue-green colour, they are classified by Italians as among the *pesce azzurro*, or blue fish, along with sardines and mackerel.

Alborella / *Freshwater Fish*
This is a very common freshwater fish, mostly found in Lake Como, which grows up to 20 cm (8 inches) in length and has a silvery skin. It is easily scaled and skinned and the flesh has a sweetish taste. The fish is often air-dried to make the speciality of Lake Maggiore, *missoltit*.

Aliotide and Patella Reale / *Limpet*
Limpets are single-shelled molluscs, looking like small pyramids, which are found attached to rocks. You need to have good eyes to spot them and a knife with a pointed tip to detach them. As long as it has come from unpolluted waters, you can eat this shellfish raw with just a few drops of lemon juice. Limpets have a very nutty flavour and are delicious in fish soups.

Anguilla, Bisato / *Eel*
This remarkable creature is both a sea fish and a freshwater fish. But the most impressive thing about the eel is the fact that they all begin their life in the Sargasso Sea off the American coast and within 2 hours of being hatched are transported by the Gulf Stream thousands of miles to Europe, where they are caught and speedily consumed. In Italy, these elvers (as they are called at this stage of their life) are known as *cieche* (meaning 'blind'), not because they cannot see but because they are so easy to catch that the fishermen say they are blind to the nets.

The fish that are not caught as elvers from the sea swim into freshwater lakes and rivers to spend 6 or 7 years maturing, before swimming back to their birthplace to breed and end their life. Eels from the Comacchio Valley at the mouth of the Po are especially good. There the elvers are trapped in artificial lakes when they enter the Po estuary south of Venice and are then effectively farmed until they reach maturity.

Aragosta, Astice / *Spiny or Rock Lobster, Lobster*
Of the many varieties of this crustacean in existence, the spiny or rock lobster, *aragosta nostrana*, the one without claws, is the most common. The larger darkish blue-green true lobster with claws is called astice and is similar to the American Maine lobster. The best way to cook lobster is to boil it in water, when the shell turns bright red. There is considerable debate about what is the most humane way to cook a live lobster and the current consensus seems to be that the swiftness of plunging it in rapidly boiling water is preferred. Once cooked it can be halved and, while still warm, sprinkled with good olive oil (preferably the most delicate Ligurian) and a few drops of lemon juice. Don't forget to provide your guests with the appropriate tools so they can extract the juicy meat from the claws.

Aringa / *Herring*
See page 15.

Baccalà, Stoccafisso / *Salt Cod, Stockfish*
Baccalà and *stoccafisso* are respectively salted and air-dried cod. Like herring, this is another preserved northern fish which has successfully found its way into Italian cuisine. Some attribute its introduction to Christopher Columbus, who found it in his ship's supplies when on the way to America. For a long time, in fact, stockfish was the staple diet of

navigators as it would last out long journeys. Both types of preserved cod come from the Lofoten Isles in Norway, where a whole industry and way of life have grown up around the fishing, salting and drying of cod.

Barbo / *Barbel*
This freshwater fish can be found all over Italy, where it lingers in the muddy beds of many rivers and lakes. It is a very delicate fish, with few bones, and is best eaten fried or poached. It must, however, never be eaten raw as the uncooked flesh is toxic.

Bottarga, Buttariga / *Roe of Grey Mullet and Tuna*
Bottarga is the name given to the roe of both the grey mullet (*bottarga di muggine*) and tuna (*bottarga di tonno*). The mullet roe is much smaller than that of the tuna and is pressed then cured in brine before being hung up to dry. Sicily and Sardinia are the main producers and consumers of this speciality, and there it is eaten in thin slices seasoned with lemon juice and olive oil as an appetizer, and on scrambled eggs.

The much bigger tuna roe can weigh up to 2 kg (4 lb) and is traditionally pressed into an oblong shape once cured. It is mostly used grated over pasta and eggs, the bland, accommodating flavour of which is the perfect foil for the strong flavours of the salted fish. It

commands very high prices and can only be found in the best shops.

Branzino, Spigola / *Sea Bass*
Sea bass is widely available in Italy, as it can be caught off any coast where the sea is fairly rough. It can reach up to 1 metre (3 feet) in length and 10 kg (22 lb) in weight.

Its popularity can be attributed to its delicate but firm flesh, which is enormously versatile and easy to cook. Whether boiled, baked or grilled, sea bass always delivers its promise. Because it is so well liked, this fish has to be farmed to meet the demand. This means that the size and weight of the fish can be controlled for culinary use. Wild sea bass are a wonderful silver colour, whereas their cultivated cousin is darker and never quite matches up in terms of flavour.

Calamaro / *Squid*
There is quite a lot of confusion about these very popular cephalopods, related to the octopus. They come in many varieties which look very similar and share similar preparation and cooking methods. The differences between the varieties are more to do with size and shape than taste or texture. The *totano seppia*, or flying squid, is notable for its habit of leaping from the water and gliding for some distance. Found mostly off the Ligurian coast, it is treated in much the same way as other squid, but has coarser flesh.

Squid have tube-like bodies with two fins, and a head with ten short tentacles attached. Two of these tentacles are much longer than the others and are lined with small suckers. The skin of the *calamaro* (squid) or *calamaretto* (baby squid) is generally pinkish in hue with flashes of white.

The squid carries ink in its body, which it ejects to confuse enemies when they are in pursuit. Italians, especially Venetians, have managed to prepare wonderful dishes using the black ink, *risotto nero* being perhaps the best-known.

Cannocchia, Pannocchia / *Squill Fish*
This most Mediterranean of shellfish, which vaguely resembles a langoustine, is very much an Italian affair. Especially common in the Adriatic, it lives in the sand and mud on the seabed. It can reach 20 cm (8 inches) in length and has a sort of fortified shell on its back and tail that has two black marks on it looking like a pair of eyes. This crustacean has many different names and uses, depending on the region. In Venice it is called *canoci*, in Puglia *caratiedde*, *spanocchio* in Naples and *cicala* in Tuscany.

To get at the tender meat, cut two small strips down each side of the body with scissors so that the meat can be extracted in a piece. It is mostly used in fish soups, but is also served boiled and dressed with olive oil and lemon juice.

Cannollechio, Cappalunga / Razor-shell

This is a very peculiar mollusc which has two shells shaped like an old-fashioned cut-throat razor. It lives on the bottom of sandy sea-beds and is quite difficult to fish because it sits in an upright position and the sharp shells can cut nets and hands. It is easiest to fish when the tide is low and you can pull the shells out of the sand.

Razor-shells can reach 30 cm (1 ft) in length, but the smaller ones are more tender. They can be grilled, added to fish soups or used in seafood salads. They are usually sold in bundles; go for those that are heavy for their size. To get at the meat without cutting yourself on the shells the *cannolicchi* must first be steamed open in a pan with a little olive oil and water.

Capasanta, Conchiglia di S. Giacomo, Pettine / Scallop

Many different names have been given by various Italian regions to this popular and most distinctive of shellfish.

One of the best varieties, the *canestrello* or queen scallop, is particularly common in the Venice region, where it lives on the sandy seabeds and is harvested by divers all year round.

Capone, Cappone / Gurnard

This is a strange fish that looks like a red mullet with a large head surrounded by bony scales and two very large fins just beneath the head. It lives in the sand on the seabed at various depths. There are several varieties which range from small to quite large, reaching up to 75 cm (2½ feet) in length.

The flesh is very good, tender but not too firm. Cut into steaks it can be grilled, but its best use is to flavour fish soups.

Carpa / Carp

This freshwater fish loves quiet waters, where it usually sits in the mud on the river or lake bed. There are many types of carp, the main differences between them being the number of scales on their body. They can reach up to 1 metre (3 feet) in length and attain quite significant weights.

Cefalo, Muggine / Grey Mullet

Because of its fine flavour, this is a very popular fish in Italy and is fished around every coast. Grey mullet is fond of estuaries, where it finds the best feeding grounds, so it can taste muddy and the best fish come from clearer waters. There are many varieties, but the most sought-after is the volpino, which in season has a rich roe used to make bottarga (see page 55).

Cernia / Grouper

This solitary fish lives in warm seas and reaches huge sizes of up to 1.5 metres (4½ feet). Its tasty firm, white flesh is considered a delicacy in Italy. Due to its size, it is usually fished with harpoons, and when it comes to cooking it is usually cut in slices and either grilled or braised, while other parts of the grouper are used to make a sauce to dress linguine. However, the most interesting way of cooking the fish comes from Sardinia, where the liver is used to produce an excellent sauce to accompany the roasted fish.

Coda di Rospo, Rana Pescatrice, Rospo / Angler Fish or Monkfish

This ugly fish is becoming more and more sought after by chefs all over the world. Its firm, tasty tail meat is almost completely boneless and, after cooking, it resembles lobster closely enough to be confused with it quite regularly.

With its large mouth, the monkfish is able to take quite large prey and spends much of its life skimming the seabed in search of food. It is therefore fished with a flexible rod which is weighted to reach the seabed. Monkfish grow to quite a large size, but generally only the tail is used. The large, ugly head is usually discarded in Italy, although in some parts of the world it is used to make fish stock and gelatine, for which it is excellent.

Cozza, Muscolo, Mitile, Muscioli / Mussel

One of the most common shellfish in the world, the mussel is used abundantly in Italian cuisine, especially in southern Italy and the Venetian lagoon, where what they call locally *peoci* are prodigious.

In the clear waters near Chioggia in the Venetian lagoon there is farm after farm where mussels grow on long ropes hanging from wooden frames. The farms are carefully regulated to ensure high standards of hygiene because of the susceptibility of the mussel to pollution.

When bought, mussels must be firmly closed and heavy, indicating that they are still alive and so completely fresh. Before cooking, they should be well washed under cold running water, using a knife to scrape off barnacles and the beards. Mussels which come to the surface when submerged in water should be discarded, as should those that don't open after cooking.

At one time, mussels were eaten raw like oysters but today, with the risk of contamination from pollution, it is essential to cook them.

Dattero di Mare / *Sea Date*
This mollusc, related to the mussel, is so named because it looks like a date. It is oval-shaped, usually reaching 5–10 cm (2–4 inches) in length and is a dark brown colour. The sea date lives in rocks where, by using acids from its body, it is able to form a niche in the rock which it enlarges as it grows.

Dentice / *Sea Bream*
This very popular Mediterranean fish can reach 1 metre (3 feet) in length. Its flesh is very delicate and can be cooked in any way.

In commercial terms, this fish is as important as the *cernia* or any of the other breams (see Orata and Sarago), all central players on the Italian culinary scene.

Donzella
Related to the gurnard and weever, the *donzella* is one of those colourful Mediterranean fish often used in fish soups and stews.

Gambero, Gamberetto, Gamberone, Mazzancolla / *Prawn, Shrimp*
The many varieties of prawn and shrimp belong to the same family as the lobster. Indeed one type of prawn, the *gambero di acqua dolce* (freshwater prawn or crayfish), is an exact miniature copy of the lobster and is almost as popular on the culinary scene. Other types of prawn do not have claws, although their armoured body and head have a very similar look to their larger cousins. Also like the lobster, the many natural colours of prawns, from pale orange and deep red to dark greyish-blue, all turn red when cooked. Prawns and shrimp are well loved and fished all over the world, but Mediterranean prawns have an unmatchable sweet taste and sea fragrance.

Today it is very difficult for most people to get fresh prawns, although there is some farming to supplement the locally caught supply. Huge worldwide demand means that most prawns are caught in large numbers and frozen on board enormous North Atlantic trawlers. The difference in quality between fresh and frozen prawns is great, but the world seems to have accepted the inferior product.

The smallest *gamberetti*, or grey shrimp, are usually eaten dusted in flour and deep-fried until crisp. They are so tender that often one can eat the entire thing without having to shell it.

Granchio, Granciporro, Granseola, Grancevola, Granceola / *Crab*
The crab family includes a large variety of these extremely tasty crustaceans. In Italy, the smaller variety, such as the *granchio* or sand or common crabs, are eaten in soups. The larger variety, called *granciporro*, is heavy and capable of yielding quite a lot of meat. For the best results these large crabs should be boiled while still alive, like lobsters. They need to be cooked for at least 20 minutes, then left to rest for 15 minutes in their cooking water. Spider crabs (*granseola, granceola* or *grancevola*) are prepared in a similar way. The best crabs come from Venice, as do the best recipes.

After cooking, the crab is opened by exerting pressure between the eyes until the back shell lifts off like a lid from a box. After removing the 'dead men's fingers', or gills, the meat from the body and claws is all collected along with the coral and mixed together and served dressed with some salt, lemon juice, parsley and a little olive oil. Larger spider crabs should be grilled or boiled whole, and the flesh added to a good tomato sauce for pasta.

There is a peculiar crab, called *moleca* in Venetian dialect, which is the equivalent of the American soft-shell crab. This is a male crab caught by expert fishermen during the spring and autumn when it discards its old shell and only has a new soft shell which has not hardened. Soft-shell or 'naked' crabs can be eaten whole dusted in flour and deep-fried.

Lavarello / Lake Fish
Almost every Italian lake harbours this well-known fish, also called *goregone*. It usually reaches 30 cm (1 foot) in length and its meat is very delicate. It is especially popular in Northern Italy, where it is used as an alternative to saltwater fish brought in from the coasts.

Luccio / Pike
This freshwater fish can reach a length of 1.5 metres (4½ feet) and up to 4 or 5 kg (9–11 lb) in weight. It is much sought after, especially in Piedmont, Lombardy and Veneto, for its firm white flesh. It is traditionally cooked *in umido*, i.e. braised with tomatoes, or minced to produce pâtés or fish cakes.

Merluzzo / Cod
The mild-flavoured cod is not much eaten as a fresh fish in Italy, only preserved. See Baccalà.

Murena, Grongo / Moray Eel, Conger Eel
The *murena* or moray eel is the dread of every underwater diver because when defending itself it goes on the attack and its bite is horrible as well as being poisonous. It is a solitary fish that lives in holes in rocks and can reach 1.5 metres (5 feet) in length. The eel's meat was appreciated by the ancient Romans for its fragrance and was widely used in mixed fish soups like *cacciucco*.

The *grongo* or conger eel, unlike the moray, is neither venomous nor dangerous. However, great care needs to be taken when preparing it as the raw blood is highly poisonous and it is only after it is cooked that the eel's flesh loses its toxicity. For this reason it is very important that any wound is covered when cleaning the eel.

Both the moray and conger eels are especially good when cut in slices and grilled, although great care must be taken to ensure that it is completely cooked before serving and eating. See page 28 for more on cooking eel.

Nasello / Hake
Once prepared, this fish is often wrongly identified as cod, but hake does not look like cod at all, although it does belong to the same family. It reaches up to 1 metre (3 feet) in length and large fish are sliced into cutlets before being cooked in a variety of ways. Its extremely fragile and delicate flesh is eaten all over Italy and cooked in many different ways according to regional variations.

Orata, Mormora, Marmora / Bream
All Mediterranean bream are related and, despite the differences in colour, texture, taste and general appearance, are very similar. Both the *mormora* or *marmora* (striped bream) and *pagello* or *pagro* (sea bream) are well loved in Italy. However, perhaps the best flavoured is the *orata* or gilthead, known to the French as the *daurade*, and the favoured way of cooking them is to bake them in the oven.

Ostrica / Oyster
It is very curious that this Italian *frutto di mare*, so loved by the Romans that they developed the first oyster farms, is now considered to be the French *fruit de mer* par excellence. In fact it was only after the French (and British) exhausted their own natural fishing grounds that they imported the farming know-how from Italy and made it such a primary industry that it is now France that dictates the rules of hygiene and other regulations for growing oysters.

In Italy the so-called belon or round oyster is still the best loved and is still farmed in the Adriatic Sea around Puglia, especially the town of Taranto. Of the few varieties that exist, Italians prefer the flat *ostrica piatta* and the round belon which is still eaten raw dressed with just a few drops of lemon juice.

The oyster is easily digestible and eating a dozen as an appetizer is quite normal. I remember once eating 126 small ones, but I certainly could not manage the remaining three courses or the pudding, and the proverbial effect one is said to experience after consumption was noticeable. Raw oysters should only be eaten when the shell is tightly closed, showing that the oyster is still alive.

Palombo / *Shark*

This type of shark found in the Adriatic is not much used in the kitchens of Italy any more due to the poor quality of its flesh. It still may sometimes be sold in Venice market as *vitello di mare*, or sea veal.

Pesce Persico / *Perch*

One of the most sought-after freshwater fish, the perch can reach 45 cm (18 in) in length. It is very much at home in the Northern rivers and lakes and is usually sold filleted because it is difficult to prepare due to its very delicate flesh and many back fins and bones.

Pesce San Pietro / *John Dory or St Peter's Fish*

Legend tells of how Saint Peter took the fish from the water with his hands, leaving the imprint of his fingers on its skin. He was worried about the payment of a tax but found exactly the right amount of money in the fish's mouth to pay the debt. This is how the fish got its name and is supposed to explain the presence of two black spots on either side of the body.

John Dory has extremely delicate flesh, but it is expensive because only 30–35 per cent of its total weight can be used once it has been filleted, which means that for four people you will need a large fish weighing at least 2 kg (4 lb). The flesh is prized for its firmness and flavour, making it very popular with chefs the world over.

Pesce Sciabola / *Sabre Fish*

The *pesce sciabola* really stands out when the fishermen bring their catches on board. Shaped like a large flattened eel and with a bright silver skin, it looks totally different from all other fish. Although quite common, because of its many small bones it is not much sought after for the kitchen. It is mostly used in fish stews and soups, where it is cut into chunks to impart flavour.

Pesce Spada / *Swordfish*

Swordfish reach up to 4 metres (12 ft) in length and 200 kg (450 lb) in weight. The fish is readily identified by the long sword or spear on its snout. Many are harpooned by fishermen off the coasts of Calabria and Sicily.

Polpo, Moscardino / *Octopus*

Old fishermen's tales about this creature abound and most concentrate on the power of its eight tentacles, each of which is armed with two rows of suckers for grabbing hold of its prey. The entire length of the octopus can reach anything from 50 cm (20 in) to 3 metres (10 ft). Smaller octopuses, weighing up to 200 g (7 oz), are very tender; anything over this size – and they can reach as much as 25 kg (55 lb) in weight – needs to be tenderized either by beating it with a stick or repeatedly thrashing it against rocks to break up the fibres of the flesh.

The octopus can be found easily on all Italian coasts and is very much prized. It has a strong beak in the centre of its oval body which, along with the eyes, has to be discarded when preparing it for cooking.

Razza, Arzilla / *Skate*

Skate is similar to monkfish and John Dory in that only a part of this fish is eaten, in this case the wings, or outer fins. The fish is completely flat and lives on the bottom of the seabed where it is perfectly camouflaged under the sand. Skate wings are sold skinned and only the long structural cartilage left in place. Whichever way it is prepared, it is quite delicious and highly recommended, provided you do not mind the cartilage, of course.

Riccio di Mare / *Sea-urchin*
Holidaymakers in the Mediterranean sometimes have the misfortune to tread on a sea-urchin, the fragile spines of which break at exactly the point where they enter the flesh, delivering a painful poison.

Sea-urchins are common around the whole Italian coast, but mostly come from Puglia, Calabria, Sicily and Sardinia, four areas where the water is particularly clean. As well as being enjoyed by the local population, the sea-urchins are distributed to towns and cities all over Italy.

There are many varieties of sea-urchin and the roe of most is edible. The roe is the sea-urchin's egg sac, which reaches maturity in the spring and early autumn. Two varieties of sea-urchin are particularly good, those with violet-to-dark-green spikes and those with shorter spikes of violet with a white spot at the end.

To prepare this most delicate of *frutti di mare*, cut off the bottom half where the mouth lies, using a pair of scissors or a special tool, and clean the inside to remove the black impurities. Leave the star-shaped piles of roe intact and attached to the shell then simply eat with a spoon or, as I prefer, simply lick them out with the tip of your tongue. The salty sweet taste of the eggs is so delicious that no accompaniment is needed.

Rombo / *Turbot and Brill*
Belonging to the sole family, these flat fish living partly on the seabed are both very sought after for their extremely white and firm flesh with a very delicate flavour.

The two types available in Italy are the *rombo chiodato* (turbot), which can reach 1 metre (3 ft) in length and is recognizable by its dark grey skin covered with small bony humps. The other type, *rombo liscio* (brill), has a paler smooth skin also with a less elongated body.

Salmone / *Salmon*
Italians have discovered freshwater salmon in the last few years, probably due to the fact that the farmed variety has only recently become affordable. Until now only a few Italians were familiar with salmon and then only smoked. Although it is not native to Italy, everyone from restaurateurs to private buyers makes the most of this wonderful fish.

Sarago, Sargo / *White Bream*
The Italians like to fish this much-loved Mediterranean fish all year round; it is either grilled with lemon juice and olive oil or baked. The best variety is the *Diplodus sargus*, which can reach 40 cm (16 in) in length and a weight of 2 kg (4½ lb). White bream prefers rocky seabeds with plenty of vegetation.

Sarda, Sardina, Sardella / *Sardine*
The name of this fish, actually young pilchard, probably comes from the area where it was mostly fished and known to the Romans around the Island of Sardinia. It is eaten in most of the Mediterranean countries and is almost a staple of all the coastal areas of Italy, where it is not only consumed fresh but also preserved in oil and salt like the anchovy (see page 10).

Scampo / *Crustacean*
The *scampo* is similar to a small lobster, and a very close relative of the Dublin Bay prawn or langoustine, which is mostly fished on the Adriatic Sea on the eastern coast of Italy. Indeed, a great many *scampi* recipes come from the Venice area. It is a very delightful crustacean with very sweet and tender meat, in my opinion superior to that of lobster.

They are delicious when extremely fresh and simply boiled, then dressed with good olive oil and lemon juice. Many of the *scampi* that come from the North Sea arrive frozen and the taste is lost completely. *Scampi* are used for fish soups and can be grilled and eaten cooked in salads. See also Gambero.

Scorfano / Scorpion Fish or Rascasse

As their name suggests, scorpion fish have poisonous spines that can deliver a nasty sting. They live on rocky seabeds and come in a variety of colours, from reddish-brown to black. They look quite fearsome and are not very friendly if badly handled.

However, this ugly fish has an excellent flavour and is very sought after for *cacciucco*, an excellent fish soup (see page 34). Smaller fish are best used in such soups, while the larger varieties (weighing 1 kg/2 lb or more) are wonderful steamed or poached and eaten with fresh mayonnaise.

Seppia, Seppietta / Cuttlefish

The cuttlefish has a shorter rounder body than the squid (see Calamaro, page 55) but the same number of tentacles. It has a less chewy texture than the squid, but there is much debate about which has the better flavour.

Sgombro / Mackerel

One of the most common fish in the world, the mackerel is closely related to the tuna and is one of the *pesce azzurro* or blue fish, because of its unmistakably black-striped, bluish skin. The fatty flesh is very firm and rather delicate but, once caught, it deteriorates quickly so freshness is paramount for the enjoyment of this fish.

However, because the oils in its flesh are healthy and because it is cheap and widely available, it is among the most commonly eaten fish in Italy.

Sogliola / Sole

Italians coming into my restaurant in London are always impressed by the tastiness of the sole, mainly because they believe Italian sole are the best that can be eaten. I must admit that the Italian dish *fritto misto* (mixed deep-fried fish), when made with a few freshly caught prawns and *sogliolette* (small sole), is one of life's greatest culinary pleasures.

Sole is available around the whole Italian coast, including the islands. There are many types of sole, which can be easily distinguished from other species of flat fish by the fact that both eyes sit on what would have been the right side of the fish.

The Dover sole lives on the sandy seabed and is so well camouflaged that it is almost impossible to see. It is fished commercially and is so heavily exploited that it is feared that stocks are seriously depleted.

Storione / Sturgeon

This large fish, common to the Black and Caspian Seas, used to live in the River Po in Italy. Now, because of pollution however, they have died out there.

The sturgeon is valued both for its eggs, which are eaten as caviar, and its fatty but very delicate flesh. In Sicily, farmed sturgeon are delicately smoked. The largest sturgeon is known as beluga in Russia and can reach up to 8 metres (33 ft) in length and about 1,000 kg (1 ton) in weight. Imagine how much caviar it can produce.

The flesh of the smaller sturgeon, about 3 kg (6½ lb), is eaten grilled, fried, stewed, baked and steamed, accompanied with various sauces.

Tartufo di Mare / Sea Truffle

This mollusc is believed by gourmets to be the perfect *frutto di mare*. It is fished with a comb, which drags up all the shells buried in the sandy seabed. Its shell is similar to that of the clam but, unlike that more common mollusc, it is both very meaty and tender. It is usually eaten raw with lemon juice, although some connoisseurs prefer it without. It is also used in a sauce to accompany linguine in a similar way to clams, or sautéed with other molluscs, see Sauté Misto di Vongole e Datteri, page 49.

Tinca / Tench

This small freshwater fish, related to the carp, lives in lake ponds and rivers. Like many such fish, unless caught from clear waters, it can have a distinctly muddy taste. Accordingly it is today not one of the most popular of fish for cooking. It is generally baked, fried or marinated in *carpione* (see page 22).

Tonno / Tuna Fish

'Tonnare' is the system of nets used by fishermen in Calabria and Sicily to catch tuna. These nets are placed in the sea in such a way as to channel shoals of tuna so that they cannot escape and they are then harpooned. It is a pretty messy way of catching fish, but one trip can produce tons and tons of tuna. The canning of tuna fish probably first came into existence as a way to cope with these sudden gluts.

When tinned, tuna fish is eaten in a totally different way from the fresh variety and can be used in sauces and *antipasti*.

Triglia / Red Mullet

There are two types of red mullet, one that has a more pronounced head and a pinkish-red skin; the other is recognized by its sleek head and its red and yellow skin. The former tastes more muddy.

Trota / Trout

The trout is probably the best-known and most common freshwater fish in Italy, which with her many lakes and rivers offers it the most wonderful habitats. However, demand still exceeds supply and farming is so common that it is almost impossible to buy wild trout. The two varieties favoured by the trout farmers are the *fario* and the rainbow. Both have wonderful firm flesh, made possible by the high quality of lifestyle reproduced in the farmed conditions.

Trout is as popular on the menus of Italian restaurants as it is with ordinary Italians. The people of the Northern regions have an especially strong tradition of cooking this lovely fish.

Vongola / Clam

Also known as *arsella* in Liguria and Tuscany, clams are small molluscs which are popularly used to make a sauce for spaghetti or linguine. They are very popular all over Italy, but especially in Naples and along the Amalfi and Adriatic coasts, where special machines are used to comb the sandy seabeds in search of them.

There are two main types, the *gialla* and the larger *vongola verace* or carpet shell clam, the latter much sought after for its better flavour and occasionally eaten raw like oysters. The *tellina* or wedge shell is said to be the best for soup.

Index

Publishing Director: Anne Furniss
Creative Director: Mary Evans
Editor: Lewis Esson
Consultant Art Director: Helen Lewis
Design: Sue Storey
Assistant Editor: Jane Middleton
Editorial Assistant: Rhian Bromage
Production: Candida Jackson &
           Vincent Smith

This edition published in 1999 by
Quadrille Publishing Limited,
Alhambra House,
27-31 Charing Cross Road,
London WC2H OLS

Based on material originally published
in *Carluccio's Complete Italian Food*.

Text © 1997 & 1999 Carluccio's Partnership
Photography © 1997 André Martin
Design, edited text and layout © 1999
Quadrille Publishing Ltd

Cataloguing-in-Publication Data:
a catalogue record for this book is
available from the British Library.

ISBN 1 899988 54 8

Printed and bound in Hong Kong.